FAITH RUN

Camino del Sol

A Latina and Latino Literary Series

FAITH RUN

—POEMS BY—
RAY GONZALEZ

THE UNIVERSITY OF ARIZONA PRESS

TUCSON

The University of Arizona Press
© 2009 Ray Gonzalez
All rights reserved

www.uapress.arizona.edu

Library of Congress Cataloging-in-Publication Data
appear on the last printed page of this book.

Publication of this book is made possible in part by the proceeds of a
permanent endowment created with the assistance of a Challenge Grant
from the National Endowment for the Humanities, a federal agency.

14   13   12   11   10   09   6   5   4   3   2   1

CONTENTS

—PART ONE—

—PART TWO—

—Part Three—

—PART ONE—

The Poem of One Hundred Tongues

The poem of one hundred tongues realigns the saxophone
until two hundred eardrums respond,

the music building into a text that wants to spill
the wine out of the conches.

The poem of one hundred tongues tattoos many faces,
the images showing mouths are outlawed.

The poem hides those faces until they open
like cactus flowers stepped on by bare feet.

The poem of one hundred tongues paints 98 faces brown,
leaving two in the sun of white, words forming

in the twins—one for truth and one for lying.
When fifty throats stop writing, the sound of dying

is mistaken for the first word.
When the other fifty throats keep writing,

light embraces everything, the sound of living
mistaken for the last word.

The poem of one hundred tongues fills the baskets at dawn,
demands a prayer to touch one hundred wet foreheads,

beads of sweat drying into moles on the skin mistaken
for periods at the end of one hundred sentences.

Trinity

I was born seven years after
the first atomic bomb, not Hiroshima,

but the one from July 1945—
Trinity Site, New Mexico,

200 miles north from where
my mother gave birth to her only son.

When I first opened my eyes,
the white sun greeted me and

I have been blind ever since.
I was born seven years too late

for the world war, though my father
served at sea before I could swim.

I have been afraid of water ever since,
though a family photo shows the war is over

and my father is young in his white uniform,
a tattoo of a blue panther rising on his right arm.

The Song

I called out, "Mama! Papa!"
I was there—people outside

the window laughing.
I whispered, "Mama! Papa!"

I thought the scene was mine.
Piano keys in a black room.

The discovered arc when love
could have been love.

I cried, "Mama! Papa!"
I touched them.

They were there.
They saw me and quit fighting.

It was a rooster atop an old dog house,
crowing as if morning never came.

I called out, "Mama! Papa!"
It was a part of my body,

a shiny stone in the glass bowl,
morning cars driving by without guilt,

no headlights to break with the past
when I finally said, "Mother, Father,"

and two strangers rose from the table
and gave me my name.

History

All my ancestors were poor and I grew
up chasing lizard tails in the dirt.

It was a small house that grew
territories in the mind.

A horse rider brought me home.
He rewrote history, then rode away.

I matured as fast as the tumbleweed.
It must have been in the canyons.

I was taught not to believe in majestic
endings, but I could still save you.

I remember my cousin hit me.
I almost drowned when we went swimming.

I grew up listening to distant train whistles.
I could show you where one derailed.

Not all of my ancestors are dead.

Somewhere Outside El Paso

Somewhere outside El Paso there is a mountain
that marks the place where it happened.

This mountain is full of canyons and cliffs
that hide their rocks well, the road into

their red space the last line drawn
before it happened.

There is a cottonwood tree that shadows
the spot where it took place.

The tree is dying, its gray trunk opening
like the arms of a witness, the empty

branches drawing the sky.
A monument cracks under the weight

of the concrete cross, the broken slab hiding
its language in the dirt so the sun moves

in the opposite direction without giving
away its secret messages.

Somewhere outside El Paso, a man watches
the tree fall on the other side of the cross,

then finds his way down to the river,
bows down, and takes a drink.

Heaven

Heaven slips into the shadows
of the men, and America begins.

Heaven streams into the hearts
of these men, and America continues.

The red walls at San Lorenzo bleed for
the highway of men, and no one forgets America.

Heaven razor-wires around the chests of these
men, who tire of burning tattoos on their backs.

Heaven is the sweat they pray to when
the brown walls at San Cristobal shelter

the image of a saint because America
wishes it could believe in miracles.

Heaven pours into the river that keeps men
from crossing, and America stays over there.

Heaven becomes a family with a father on
that side, but American children over here.

Heaven is the women who answer men
by lying down to fill American soil.

The blue walls at San Ignacio hide their children
because heaven is the chant they memorize

late at night and into their morning sleep.
Heaven is the crumbling border on the map

that was never drawn because these men walk
on a desert highway leading to a horizon

absent of people because heaven is
the steel fence that is never there.

Moon Yard

Carlos, what do you see
when the trails turn to gold?
Which direction leads to
the yanked heart, the guitars
that sound like they love us?
Even the mice in your aquarium
are waiting to die, but you don't
know how to feed them.
Where did the moon go
before we saw it?
When men crossed the street
in the night, you couldn't wake
from your soliloquy to the desert,
barbed-wire heaven where others
wait for you to untie their feet
as the swaying moon beams
thousands into a country that
hesitates to give them a home.

Carlos, what does it mean?
Old people are dying
and there are no answers
to their riddles, the desert rain
mistaken for burned empanadas
no one baked.
When you fled, you melted
the Spanish candles and formed
words in English, stood in
the doorway and waited for
the jaguar to cross the street
and do damage before it
blessed your sleeping children.
You haven't been the same since,
your moon hair falling out before
your children could grow their own.

Carlos, is it true that the light
we choose is the light that turns
us away, as if the black horizon
leads to a garden where things grow
as you kneel there each day,
wondering why you feel like
a fool on your knees, until
the moon turns black in
the yard of your grief,
inside our riddled homes where
we cry when the moon burns
too close to our eyes?
Carlos, you have lifted from
our hands like the last soldier
to die across the sea.
Look at us and count to three—
one for the moment we found out,
two for the mistake of our weaknesses,
and three for the moon that moves
at dawn without warning us
it will return.

The Arrival

after Li-Young Lee

The boy arrives in the desert
and burns his feet.
He is not the boy who
was born here, but the boy
who died in this place.

The boy arrives and does not die again.
He walks on blistered feet, moving
toward the mountains that look alike.
The boy does not know why the heat

of the sand has changed his skin.
He walks because the house is gone,
leaves cold fires along the border,
the smoke healing his awful feet.

            *

When I arrive, I am not the boy.
I am too old, and my parents
much older, the house where they
used to hide still standing,
although smoke spreads its arms
across the walls as it has done for years.

The smoke spells something I can't
comprehend, though the ancient
bricks reveal a proud face,
a look that frightens me into
thinking I should not return.

When I arrive, I have been
one man, but the other man
acts like a little boy when the first
rain falls and soothes his wrinkled feet.

When I arrive, I laugh at
the shadow of black hands
someone drew on the wall of the house.
I laugh because the outspread palms
were the last things I saw when
I left thirty years ago.

                    *

The boy leaves the door open.
Fingers of ash have been wiped
from its lone window.
The boy leaves the door open,
and God wants to answer him,
but his god disappeared in
the canyon of the dead,
and the markings on the cliffs
were not drawn by him.

The boy leaves the door open.
Fingers of ash appear
in the arroyos, the rain unable
to wash them away.
The boy leaves the door open,
and his god touches the mountain walls.

                    *

When I saw what arrival was
about, I was terrified because
I believed I had never left,
though the open house wilted
beyond the desert heat and flew
across the Jornado del Muerto
years ago, splintering into a cloud
mistaken for a dust storm.

When I saw what arrival
would involve, I stepped
here instead of there,
found myself breathing hard
and staring at crossed antlers
high in the cottonwood tree,
then I looked down at blossoming
mud flowers that adorned my feet.

*

The boy arrives and begins to sing.
He has songs about love and brothers,
cooking ovens and the silent sister.
The boy gets there and keeps singing,
though the song includes the story
about the hidden scorpion, twelve
black widows, and the mighty
Gila monster embedded in the rocks.

The boy arrives and is mute and wise.
He sees the door is closed, though
the song always parts the deepest
layers of ash left by the burned
fingers the boy accepted when
he scorched his father's guitar.

*

I arrive and don't know what year it is.
I get there and tell too many lies.
I join the jagged peaks and pretend
the road up there has always been
the path I was shown by the last
man who got off the train,
the depot in El Paso destroyed
in the revolution, the invading
horses leaving marks on my forehead,
though my face belonged to my

grandfather, who was forced to fight
on Pancho Villa's side, this memory
blood invisible like the idea that
someone waits for the boy
with a love that burns each time
the boy leaves the door open
and defies the cooling rains.

Not Today

The blue jar shattered into
an open eye wishing glass stars
were fires of the conversation.
You did not hear the question.
There was a pink rose,
a tattooed heart, and a drawing
of an abandoned car on a bridge.
The smoke from the forest stayed,
though you were summoned too soon.

You had to wear the necklace,
though it was not the time for
long hair, but for jazz,
the idea that trapped you
inside the walls of yesterday.
You recalled the smell of
the fugitive, the encircled light
pretending it was blood left from
a story you could not finish
because the clock ran out of time
in his empty apartment.

The blue jar kissed you with cold
fingers that felt like a summer song
you forgot when you became
the tiger in a torn comic book.
When the fragile, yellow pages
fell out, you were a paper leaf.
When the artifacts of memory
disintegrated into nothing,
you were simply the signature in
fading ink.

Chosen

It was an emblem of a creature tattooed
on the forehead of a boy I knew in
the years of the broken neighborhood,

the youth falling in the street during the rain,
whispering it was my turn, though
my head glistened in the sun as well,

summer days of Kool-Aid and dark
rooms steaming into a sidewalk where
the branded boy waited to guess my name.

It was the 110-degree heat, waves melting
the kid into a symbol on the side of a house
I never entered, his mother dead long ago,

his father a stain on the tree outside the door,
the furnace of the street keeping me back
as the creature sweated on the boy's face.

I saw what he meant when he stole my toys,
promising he would give them back when
I could spell his name and touch his face

as if I knew what lost grandfathers know—
it is wrong to trace the burning vein on
brown skin, wrong to pretend love is desire,

each try at crossing the street a chance to save
the boy by holding him in the rain, patterns
of mud returning my broken toy soldiers to me.

The Cardboard Box

I played in a large box as a child,
found it on the living room floor one day,

the box not as big as the kitchen stove,
or one that held clothes for Goodwill.

The cardboard was stained, smelled
like blood, as if that explains why

I climbed in and sat inside, the flaps open,
light from the windows keeping me there,

my imagination taking me on a canoe across
a river that led to a cave where I put my hands

on walls covered with symbols
I would not know until years later,

a sudden lack of air making me
crawl out of the box in a panic.

I sat on the floor catching my breath,
looked around the empty room,

rose and kicked the cardboard, sent my foot
through the side, the box springing across

the floor as if it were alive. When it settled,
I went to it and climbed back inside.

Patience

Three weeks before I woke up,
birds came to visit my father.

When the birds alighted near his hair,
I was his son, but he was already dead.

I took his place because those sparrows,
finches, and the cardinal came for me.

Two weeks before I woke up,
the clay mask fell off the wall

and shattered into tiny pieces,
its two eyes becoming one

deep hole in the floor.
As I swept it up, the pain

in my chest was severe.
I lay down in a second bed

because my father
was in the first.

One week before I woke up,
I found I could sleep with

a quiet rhythm among
the waiting flowers.

When I opened my eyes,
the dirt on the bed was mine,

and the leather jacket hanging
in the closet was my father's.

Wearing the Reptile Shirt

Wearing the reptile shirt, he is mistaken
for a good boy, his tail left behind in his

dresser drawer, its magic reserved for those
who truly believe. Wearing his skin, he wanders

the streets without a name or gifts.
He knows he is immortal and gives

credit to his reptile shirt.
Wearing it, he is a silent youth

with dark wisdom who hisses
at things he doesn't like.

Putting on his layers, he hides among
parked cars and appears unnoticed at rear

windows as sweaty couples wrestle inside,
the peeking son with reptile skin keeping

lovers together or breaking them up.
Disappearing after desire, he wishes

he could breathe in a bare chest, but can't
stop wearing the reptile thing

because without it he would be a boy again.
He can't forget the reason for disguise

before going forth, his identity bound
to hidden things and rapid movement,

his clamoring across trees and sleeping
houses forming the myth as he returns

to his room each night and meets his dreams
before the reptile shirt becomes the dirty

sheet on his bed his mother
changes each morning.

Drive

Bobby and Roy Williamson called me
"dumb Mexican," and "fat, brown
greaser" as I walked home from school,
staying ahead of them because my neighbors
loved to pound me on the arms for kicks.
We crossed the arroyos, a dirt trail
the shortcut to our homes—
a highway by the school jammed
with students staring out car windows
at boys who dropped into the desert
until the first one climbed out of
the rocks because he wanted to run.

My father got me a junk station wagon
for 200 dollars, and Bobby and Roy
got morning rides, chanting, "Drive!
You dumb Mexican! Drive!"
I gripped the wheel, braked slowly
at stop signs, dreaming of forgetting
to look both ways. I did look,
though I never saw them after
school when I drove home because
there were too many students
and it wasn't cool to jump
into a beat-up car whose
driver was smarter than you.

Halfway through high school,
I got Gary, a bully, to beat
the crap out of Bobby.
His face was smashed into
a bloody pulp, the circle of boys
at the park jeering and getting hard,
the punk beating Bobby, who said

"Yes" to a challenge built on a lie
because, when I wasn't driving,
I was lying to Gary about awful
things Bobby said about him.
My neighbor cleaned up at my house
after the beating, couldn't go home
in shame, his swollen face the amulet
I wanted to hang on my rearview
mirror each time I drove to school.

I don't know what ever happened
to those guys.
Bobby and Roy quit riding with me
not long after the beating.
I feared retaliation for a long time,
though they never found out.
My station wagon broke down,
disappeared along with Bobby,
Vietnam I think, 1970.
Strangers live across the street now,
and I sometimes wait to hear
"Spic! Chuy!" when I visit my mother
and stare at the house across the street,
knowing there is no one there
when I drive up.

Honking at the Cemetery

He drove his drunk buddies into
the cemetery one night, parked his car
in the middle of the gravestones,
their giggles stopping when he honked
the horn in the middle of the dead,
pressed his elbow into the metal ring
on the steering wheel and signaled
to his father to rise from the ground
and whip him again, his friends begging
him to start the engine and get them
out of there when they heard something
call back, not a shout or a scream,
but a note from an ancient instrument.
He claimed, later, he honked all the way,
drove slowly down the path between
the markers, the sound they heard
in the trees not the dying echo from
his horn. He paused at the gates,
looked both ways before entering
the highway to deliver the boys,
dodging the oncoming lights at
the last second the way the old man
taught him during moments between
fathers and sons when every blinding
beam in their eyes counts.

By Summer

By summer the air will leave an afterword,
and this absence will unknot the grasses,
open them to waters that carry the moon.

By the hands that feed the soil
and the shadows that close eyelids,
there will come an answer.

In the dawn of the flyway and
the rotting path to the adobe wall,
the child will turn away from the truth.

Upon the fading signature in the fields
and beside the red mountains of faith,
the rains will, at last, punish the cemeteries.

Finished House

When I walk home, the house
is heavy with fruit, the trees
lighted with blossoms.
When I walk home, the pictures
are framed on the walls,
the key in the door.
This is the house of mistakes
and clothes, a burning kitchen,
a foundation for cemented feet
and secret stories, a place
that survives the trees.
I see my pet pigeon at age seven,
the lightning strike in the backyard,
a sweating, pregnant belly,
recall my brother who goes unnamed,
the guitar leaning at the foot of the stairs,
friction between the mountain and sky,
how I carved my initials on the rocks
in the backyard garden.

Now, the earth opens and sparrows fall through.
The earth opens and my pet pigeon falls in.
When the earth closes, the town changes
its name and the river flows,
though the house is still there.
The earth closes and I put my clothes on.
The earth shuts and I wear
suspenders for the first time.
My shoes are worn and I learn,
though my arms are sore and I grow.
My hamburger is done and I eat.
When I enter my room,
the transistor radio comes on.
When I enter my room, the bed
is unmade and I leave.

Walking away is good and I know
why I come back and the cottonwood
never falls, why the magician makes
the bridge collapse as I tie my shoes.
This is the reason for staying awake,
a clue to the boarded windows,
the lesson that leaves a sliver of paradise,
but invites me to comb my hair.
This is how I shave each day,
collect postcards that don't lie,
love what I have.
This is the way the rattlesnake strikes,
misses me, and I hear something else,
mistake the night for a stain trailing
the cut belly of a rejected god.
I have cousins I never see.
They don't visit the finished house
and I am sad, my high school buddies
killed in Vietnam long ago.
My destiny is history and I run,
the dark fields actually leaves and branches,
though my writing hands are brown.
I am visited by a walking cane,
as if I know how to go,
why I am rejected by a tribe with
three painted figures on their jars.

Again, the earth opens, the ventriloquist
climbs up, and I tell myself not to listen.
The earth opens with the moon
and sun misspelled.
The earth opens and the worm
falls into the drinking glass.
The earth closes when my hands move.
The earth closes, eats the Mexican border,
and the desert becomes snow.

The earth closes and I lose my rosary,
though I am taught well.
When I walk home, I am afraid.
When I walk home, a man has water
drip onto his forehead,
his front yard landscaped and complete.
When I walk home, mailboxes explode
and the neighbors finally agree
it is my finished house.
When I walk home, a fresh pair
of socks waits for me, though
my favorite pen has dried out.
When I walk home, my love
asks me a question and I water
the garden for good luck.
When I enter my home, sparrows
fly up and I count them.

My City Is Full of Insects

after Federico García Lorca and Victor Hernández Cruz

My city is full of insects.
They bristle inside my brain
because I walked down the wrong street,
their wings twisting my tongue until
I started thinking all over again.
My city is full of insects because
I was born in the wrong house,
this idea escaping my throat because
beetles buzz the air, the constant fly
circling my head as if it owns my eyes
and wants to spring down
my open mouth.

My city is full of insects
and I live in the unpaved streets,
sand mixing with fire ants that
love my legs, the stings and blisters
sending me flying over the houses.
My city is full of insects because
freedom is about the *cucaracha*
crawling up my arm as it disappears
inside my chest.
When I scratch from wisdom and want,
the *cucaracha* comes apart, its brittle
legs falling off my tongue.
I spit strange, smart words in
the dirt that leads to the house
where the scorpions were born.

My city is full of insects because
dust clouds from old days
refuse to blow away,
mosquitoes hovering in the sewers,
the alleys, even in the water in
the sink where my head was dunked
until I came up coughing, throwing
up the last piece of paper I swallowed
after I swatted the *garapata* that survives
the poem on the page, the lice of time
mistaken for the germs of tomorrow
when my city cures itself of insects by
spraying fumes of magic I must escape.

The Rio Grande Near Flood Stage, Summer 2006

You can't forget a river before crossing it.
—A stranger

When I crossed it, I was home.
When I stayed home, I was close
but could not count the cracks
in the adobe walls.
The less I say about cracked walls,
the more you will know.
I crossed the water
and the bridge was still there.
I made it to the other side
and didn't know where to go.
When vulture shadows painted
the town from overhead,
I wasn't there.
This was long ago, when people
left the dirt streets dying
and singing, the muddy
waters changing course.

I wandered past the river,
was given bread and medals
but was never allowed to wash
and find a place to sleep.
When I crossed again,
I was lost.
When I left, a man over
my left shoulder picked up
a white stone and I saw
the river stretch where
neither one of us
could cross.

The more I traced the current,
the closer the mountains rose.
The darker the river grew,
the farther I walked
in search of a way to
find the other side.
Someone followed me
and disappeared by the bridge.

He must have been the man
who told me to never pause
before a river without taking
a drink or two.
When I understood, I could not
lower my lips to the brown water.
It dripped and glowed off
my open palms.
It was the last time the flood
would come, the drops
from my hands forming
tiny patterns on my shoes.

What We Love

I was considering becoming
an old man, but it is what
I love about the years of asking
too many questions, as if that
crow wants to leave my yard
before I tap on the window
to frighten it away, this silly
act what I love about not
knowing enough.

Robert Desnos once wrote that
a spring morning means
we are all well dressed.
Well, I am not well dressed
because it is love for conducting
the bird symphony that takes place
around my house, as if those
robins chasing a squirrel from
their nest had something bigger
to love than my green yard.

I was thinking about this love
when a cardinal landed in
the cherry tree, its red flash lasting
for an instant before it left.
Seconds later, another crow
flapped into the grass and bowed
its black head, searching for worms
I spot each morning, pink strings
rolling across the driveway
because what we love is not here
but over there, waiting for us to
be smart enough to sit under
the wet tree and give it a name
as we throw seeds.

The Shortest Poem

The shortest poem is about love
and the blue jay in the backyard,

though the red cardinal wakes us each morning.
The shortest line is about loss and not

about the red wings of memory,
or the hummingbird appearing before

the mud wasp nest on the windowsill,
hovering over it for a few seconds,

its quick disappearance unnoticed
by the fist of bristling wasps, even though

the shortest poem is about love
and not about our closed eyes,

uncertain the hummingbird
was ever there.

Roadside Shrine, Las Cruces, New Mexico

The cross divides the highway
between heaven and earth.
When clouds burst against
peaks of the Organ Mountains,
Don Benito crossed the road,
following the shadow that appeared
to him each morning.
His long beard came from
the sign he made before
the asphalt moved.
When the sun burst against
the mountains, he was marked
with flowers, his name
mounted on wires that hummed
with each passing car.

The desert rain lights everything
that winds through the canyons,
the white cross at the side
of the road erected higher
than the peaks of sleep,
the image of something
at the side of the highway
making some drivers notice,
though one of them flashes by
and makes the sign of the cross,
the release of the wheel sending
the vehicle toward the arroyo
that opens when the world arrives.

The Long Library

In the long library, I found the clay bowls.
They were stacked in dust, hundreds of them

on shelves that changed the horizon.
I wanted to touch the ancient jars

but was held back by an air that hit my lungs,
and I saw the hands of the people

would hold the stored jars
until the world came to an end.

In the long library, I unrolled parchments that
confused me with stick figures running for their lives.

I stared at events I was not supposed to witness,
and I dropped the past into glass containers.

In the long library, I read maps left behind by
men who couldn't cross the river without looking

at the black trees they did not mark, their maps
showing there is more than one way out.

In the long library, I fingered statues cold to the touch,
their twisted faces melting into my palms like a warning

that I had gone too far, the hallway behind me whispering
that I could step across and become something I was not.

In the long library, I found the passage I had been looking for.
It read, "Things you leave out in the rain reappear inside.

Mountains you carry in your pocket turn to dust
at the end of the dirt road."

In the long library, I closed the yellow book,
crossed the hallway and paid the fee to step outside.

—Part Two—

Walt Whitman's Eyeglasses

If Walt Whitman's secret poem could be
believed, fathers and sons held a ceremony
on a battlefield where black clouds
covered their faces in bruises their
women could heal with kisses.
If he was here, heroes and villains
would gather in the square to examine
Whitman's eyeglasses, passing them from
man to boy, until they saw the truth.

If I could see, I would find Whitman
walking down the street without his
spectacles, blinded in the sunlight
where young boys hide themselves,
waiting to run to a figure they know
from portraits they were given on
the night their fathers left.
If I could have his eyeglasses, I would gently
reach for the milky frames, possession of
the brittle wires left out of the poem
where he wrote it was time for someone
to put them on and take a look.

You Shall Serve

Pablo Neruda fled Chile on horseback,
going into exile to see how the snow peaks

got in the way of Federico García
Lorca's ascent to heaven.

When he paused at the edge of the world,
Neruda found the prison gate that opened

when Miguel Hernández lifted away,
dying cities in his skeletal palms marking

the path for the Spanish man to sit upon
the crown of his father and pray.

An Apache crossed the train tracks to hand
your grandfather a token of his escape,

the passing of a white stone into his hands
marking Bonifacio for the rest of his short days.

When the stone rolled off his deathbed,
your mother caught it, swears to this day

only a girl of thirteen could reach out
and pluck her father's rock out of the air.

Robert Frost visited his daughter in the insane
asylum, madness in the dark woods surrounding

a wooden fence with branches that gorged
upon the ice until the barn gave way.

When Frost walked through the trees,
he stumbled upon a frozen milk can,

kicked it out of the way so he could
run without having to look behind him.

The white stone turned gray, then black
over the decades, your mother refusing

to add it to the jar of rocks you collected
as a boy, setting the heavy container

upon a Red Chief writing tablet as
a gift on your thirteenth birthday.

Decades later, you ran into Larry Levis at the foot
of the stairs, the young poet burning with fame,

the bottle of bourbon slipping out of his arms
as he stumbled to the second floor, though

the crowd he had to address was downstairs
where their mute faces waited for his words

at a retreat near mountains that refused
the snows that year, a gathering of translators

offering Neruda and Miguel, tall rooms of papers
and books turning into cliffs and gorging rapids

after the conference when you rode the raft down
the Colorado River and almost fell in, Larry offering

homage to the exiled poor, his sentences left
behind when hundreds of white stones pounded

the cabins of the poets that cold night,
waking them to start counting the dead.

Reading: Late Summer

after Charles Wright

The morning cicadas won't stop.
When I look out the window, the willow hides
their location near the neighbors' barking dog.

James Wright wanted his horses to blossom,
the roadside littered with remains of his life.
Pablo Picasso entered caves to paint over

primitive men's marks, admitting
it was wrong to be so mortal
in the eyes of angry gods.

The walls of my garage are covered in webs
absent of their creators, bags of trimmed branches
waiting for disposal, forming more places for spiders.

Robert Lowell's long, white hair resembles
my father's, but too many summers have passed
for the old poet to write another letter

describing how he touched the light
and the voices tortured his head
to deliver a poem into his hands.

I stare at the Jimi Hendrix poster in my
office, the latest biography revealing how he was
thrown out of the Army to go burn his guitar.

The morning is cooler than I thought.
The early chill hides what I can't know—
where is the key to the surge in men,

so they can make their way to the curious stars?
Who can evolve with passion when rows of books
collect dust and smell as the year progresses?

When Eugenio Montale wrote a poem to his
mother, he claimed there were red lilies
everywhere, even in the cane breaks that

lined the water in her final days, red everywhere
as the color of warning and love, streaks of it
on boulders as I made my way up Mount

Cristo Rey thirty-five years ago, climbing with
pilgrims, trying to reach the concrete cross at
the top to stay in the church, my first poem

a few years from creation, the trek up
the hot mountain at twenty-two showing me
how to leave the arches to cross the river

like a man who would grow old and afraid,
the cross never reached, Octavio Paz admitting
his loss for words as his mother rose out

of her tomb, reached with her hands to bless him,
whispering to him that the language of mercy is dead.

The Lizard

after Elizabeth Bishop

The eye crawls out
of the stone cup,
swims across the river
to give up the need to see,
its armor of green flesh
open to the idea of sin.
It is not sin, but the rocks
settling into the ferns
where no man thinks
and no woman dreams.

If the lizard on the rock
ceases to live, there will be
a way to flee without
looking back, the slashing
tail as troubling as the comet
that hit the desert
to open a hole
no one has seen.

The mind's crown is
a hat of bitter clouds,
fire, and reptilian need—
the pierced body of
the dead man disappearing
into logs that float
to the end of the world,
where the hiss of the lizard
is the human heart
opening to a sound
it does not fear.

Juárez Bees

They swarm in the tower of the church
of La Virgen de Guadalupe, then fly out
of the belfry in a cloud of miracles.
The Tarahumara Indian woman with no legs
looks up from her wooden platform on wheels,
the sky turning the color of her hair.
The Juárez bees can't find the border or
escape the humming heat where captured
young men float down the Rio Grande.
The Tarahumara in the plaza searches for
the air of the bees, their humming
transformed into the stumps that used
to be her knees, until she feels her feet
have returned after being crushed
for forty-six years. She looks down,
but her torn skirt covers what is left.
She knows her feet.

A hair full of bees descends into
the crowded streets, people running
and screaming as the bees flash in lines
of blue and electric wind, the rest of
the swarm following the river for a few
miles, then turning back to the church.
The Juárez bees enter the church in
the evening, red light of the setting sun
igniting the air with sounds the Tarahumara
recalls from her days as a little girl who
used to stick her hands in the rich
honeycombs of San Luis Potosí,
her dripping fingers blessing her face
with the sweetness of honey and
a body no one could break.
The church is now locked at night,

the bees settling in the bricks as
the woman rolls down the sidewalk
among the people strolling in the square,
their dropped coins sparkling in the street.

Bob Dylan in El Paso, 1963

Bob Dylan passed through my hometown
to cross into Juárez, Mexico.

He used the Stanton Street bridge that
arched over the river and led to the red lights.

When he sang, "They got some hungry
women there, and they'll really make a mess

out of you," my buddies and I knew the place,
the high school ritual of having to go there

to find Dylan and his shadow going upstairs.
Dylan must have had breakfast somewhere

in El Paso, because you could never cross
without a good set of *huevos* and tortillas

churning inside you, ready to explode in
the sunrise colors of a frontier dream.

Dylan sang, "When you're lost in the rain
in Juárez and it's Easter time, too,"

and I searched for the mission where
he might have knelt and prayed, entered

to find statues of saints draped in dark
colors like a waiting concert stage.

It didn't matter that he was Jewish, because
all men going into the Juárez night

have to kneel and pray sometime.
Dylan sang, "I started out on burgundy,

but soon hit the harder stuff," and
I bought a bottle of mescal in Juárez

for him, the worm at the bottom of
the round jar still there after 45 years,

the black liquid churning dreams Dylan
had when he entered The Cave, the name

of the legendary cantina etched on
tamale leaves Dylan left on his plate.

Bob passed through my hometown
after he left Juárez.

His shadow is still there, appearing every
now and then in profile on the mountain

surrounding the town, the only El Pasoans
who know it is him growing fewer in number

because the silver raven has taken many of
them away, though there is a rumor

The Cave is still open for business,
the women waiting, the most popular

bedroom half paradise–half museum
because one of the dirty adobe walls has

writing in faded lipstick that says,
"Zimmerman Was Here."

Chimayo, New Mexico

The wooden cross stopped us in our tracks,
trees swaying so we could see.

The conductor of light blessed us with
lies to influence our dreams where

we were nameless until the flash
signaled it was permissible to cross.

The symmetry of one branch folded an
ornament of spring, easy time under heaven

and beyond plague, a scattering of thoughts
begging our sons to let us into the sanctuary.

Entering made us into silhouettes of what
grew in the valley over years of uncovering

the owl mask that never blinked
as it taught us sorrow and patience,

how faith was revived as we entered and knelt
to find a twig in the palm and a claw in the sand,

cutting to the day we hid in the groves,
moss around the trees meaning the rain had ceased.

This return was a step into flowers where passion is enough,
the mission rising in mist without opening its door,

a riddle mistaken for souls allowed to flee,
until flight is a ruined building forgotten on the earth,

voices inside keeping us from whispering
that it was the singing that made us return.

Ears Full of Thorns

The music of silence was composed
when Santa Fe fell in 1619,
Pueblo people cutting off
the heads of the Spaniards.
The angels who guided
the conquistador betrayed him
and left him to die in the canyon.
The wolf believed in rosaries,
chewed a bundle of them
before he was shot in
the season of faults.

My brother never woke from
the umbilical cord around his neck.
The music of loss and defeat
is the beauty composed during
the shattering of the clay ovens.

My streets were lined in brown
when mud was legal and no one
felt they had to put iron bars
in every window.
Waiting for the signal to attack,
Juan Carlos Arrete entered heaven
by welcoming the spear that
inflated his body and set him on
the black horse he rode as a boy.

There is no mercy when
the rat leaves the hole and
a Gila monster emerges instead,
its black body dotted in pink,
its ugly head flashing its tongue
to see if the blood of

our waiting had dried.
What binds us is a passageway
to the jars of salt where
my grandmother diminished
our history by chanting to
the badger and the coyote
mounted on the wall.

The notes of darkness and
headaches are the song of
a passing truck full of
migrant workers on the way
to slow deaths, the fields
of cotton and chile destroyed
by the black fumes that
took over the valley.
The mouth of judgment
is a shoeless foot.

When Cochise erased
the markings on the rocks,
twenty-eight of his warriors
were killed by the Mexicans.
When Emiliano Zapata was gunned
down in conspiracy, three white
stallions were set free in
the town square by his enemies.
When André Breton found
a plate of blue feathers by
his cot in the Zuni pueblo,
he wrote seven poems and
crossed the desert on foot.
When a tiny lizard was eaten
by the boy on a dare,
his friends stared at him
and walked away for good.

The ear bristles with love,
but no one listens to the choir
because the moment of bowing
down is covered in purple
curtains thrown on the bodies.
My turn consists of taking a twig,
tying a blade of grass around it,
then holding the twig in the air
for a falcon to take.

Garapata

Rooms and mud cells breed rumors of saints
passing through walls to bless the empty plates,

the great dismay of the Spanish horses ending
in arrows on the banks of the Río Puerco.

Perhaps Robert Oppenheimer's riding hat is
a part of this, his lab at Los Alamos turning whiter

with each hair he yanked out of his head.
No one feared the mushroom cloud except him.

Generations south of Socorro were born
with that Trinity bruise, the Trinity eye,

a swollen mark following them into
the caves where everyone was fed.

Even the fat man selling tacos on the corner of
Paisano and Stanton got a chance to tell it like it is—

his grandfather almost shot Pancho Villa in 1913,
but the General fired first, missed, and ran down El Paso Street

to become a shadow the fat man bows to each time
a customer burns his tongue on a thousand chile seeds.

The cottonwoods have disappeared, their
trajectories marking the sky with a burning

ash that harvests everything between Chamberino
and the volcanic hole at Missing Springs.

When you last fell into it, your face glowed
red for days, the black marks on your fingers

allowing you to sketch the history of stick
men across chambers that never gave way,

entrapping those figures in a dirt cloud
for an eternity no one can experiment with,

your climb out of the hole marking your skin
with something only sunlight can forgive.

Faith Run

Angels instead of music posters.
A stand-up bass instead of a violin.
The broken wheel, the shining stone,
a blonde wig, the desperate message

hidden in the need to go underground
and not reappear until the war ends.
Idealistic weather, idealistic guitar,
friends who believe in their fate.

Angels instead of music posters of
dead rock stars. Men with heavy
voices opening umbrellas on sunny days.
French poets ignoring the moon.

Young lovers afraid of the future, denying
they have already crossed the street.
Dictionary defining what a sleeping bag is,
clarifying what a body bag is for.

Angels instead of music posters of dead
rock stars pointing with their instruments.
The differences between two men settled
with a chess game. Belief pounded by

a nun with a stick onto the head of a boy.
The narrative on the alley wall coming alive
to change the history of the neighborhood
as excited boys take over.

The first Greek ship spotted in the library.
Significance of the thriving bamboo forest
lost when the thirsty scientist finds
the ancient walls sticking out of the ground.

Simple irony in Hernan Cortes forcing
Moctezuma to turn on his people.
Key note in George Custer being one of the first
to go down at the Little Bighorn.

Angels instead of music posters of dead
rock stars pointing their instruments at the crowd
and choosing groupies for the night.
A primitive, lyrical impulse never making it
to the floor of composition because the jaw
bone smashed the composer on the head
and sent him to the amplified stars.
Volcanic snow and mirrored hand-grenades.

The three-legged dog. The surviving tadpole.
A diminished circus clown sitting in his dressing
room, unable to wash off his face paint.
An age where book pages are never turned.

A time where computers are never turned on,
the nightmare of a blank screen affecting
the young writer's cyber habit.
Last night's virus hiding and waiting.

Announcements never made.
A basket of ham sandwiches backstage.
The boy touching the girl there for the first time.
The acquaintance leaving town to get married.

Flowers marked for the Catholic saint, rain starting
to fall before he can bless people. Calm franchised
and bottled to be delivered to heroes hiding inside
combat radios while angels wash their oil-stained wings.

Angels instead of music posters of dead
rock starts pointing their instruments at the crowd
and choosing their groupies for the night
the moment before the crowd riots.

Photo of Pablo Picasso with His Shirt Off

The hairy chests of men always get in the way.
You can love the bald approach, though

it will kill you when the world sees
your painting is the keyhole to the other

world where men's nipples are actually
dark moon craters on secret maps

woven into their shirts.
The hairy look of genius gets in the way.

You can smear the paint on your cheeks
and say it was madness, broken love,

some idea of fame that made you create.
When history enters the burned museum,

they will find you there, your shirt on,
the buttons gleaming like the stars.

The hairy chests of men will get in the way.
You will worship the brilliant stroke, the act,

a charcoal bull snorting and tossing itself into
your heart, making you finally take off your shirt

to show your chest because your sternum is
the arch sheltering the last sacrificial cave.

Allen Ginsberg's Mother

Naomi Ginsberg went insane
and never returned to her family.
So did Elizabeth Bishop's mother,
ideas of the brain twisting out
of sanitariums to feed poets
for their entire careers.

I don't know about crazy Robert
Lowell's mother, though mine
stayed home and dominated me
with the quiet grace of someone
who knew how to avoid the hallways
of grief, the madness of generations
avoided when her family worked
the railroads of Arizona instead,
the potential to lose it sweated
across the desert hills.

Ginsberg's mother roamed their
house naked, urging her son
to come closer, then screaming
at him to get away.
Bishop's mother screamed in
Nova Scotia, the icicles in her
attic breaking off the ceiling
like the words of silence
we memorize.

My mother never screamed.
She whispered and prayed
for my sins instead,
whispering, again and again,
as she pointed to my sins.
She would take her jar

of black crayons,
a dozen markers she kept
to censor and black out
the huge tits on the photos
of strippers who advertised
in the *L.A. Free Press*,
the hippie rag I subscribed to
when I was fifteen, each issue
I read smeared in black
each time she was done.

She insisted the naked body
was a sin, a cover-up, her clothes
buttoned to the neck to make sure
the cries coming out of her warm
throat were commands to a son
who would never forget.

Awake

You wake at two a.m. and the country has
lost the knife. You have two hands
and the haircut you wore in high school.
You ask God if he plays cards and the brand
of fire he drinks, wake at four a.m. when
your nephew lands in Iraq, insisting he missed
the action, his second tour igniting
a sunset over the Northern Crazies.

You can't reveal where those mountains are,
or where the stone chairs are buried from
the last war that left some men digging,
others sitting in their petrified seats.
No one wants to climb those heights.
In the tall grass of your backyard,
there is a face that blesses your house,
the national music of promised peace.

This isn't about the way you made it out
of La Mesilla Valley at twenty-three.
It is about the night you were born,
how your father was mesmerized by
a fly on the hospital wall.
Years later, on the highway to Tucson,
he spotted Mars in the night sky,
its light making him enter the mountains.
When he emerged, the fly was still on
the wall. You were already born,
your mother fed soup and crackers in
the hospital while her baby refused to cry.

After one year in-country, your nephew called
your sister to say they had to convoy to
Kuwait as the only safe place to get out.

When you woke at six a.m. in San Ignacio,
the river was a stain in your book, the Gila
monster in the walls ready to spray its
pink spots into your eyes.
When you blinked, you saw the white beard
of a man chiseled in rock who told you
there are mothers in his garden without
their sons, women on the axis of the earth
waiting for things to turn as they must do.

The Dragonfly of Death

My 20-year-old nephew calls his mother from Iraq.
He is on his second tour of duty, wants to know

if my sister has sold his old pickup truck.
He will need the money when he gets home,

wants to start over again, telling his father
he has changed his mind about going back

as a civilian to help the Iraqi people.
"There is too much death," he says on the phone.

My mother and sister cry every night, their
prayer-rosaries filling books I will never write.

*

I dreamed about the dragonfly of death four days
after Julia, my 96-year-old grandmother, died.

The dragonfly hovered with white wings,
white stars above, its body floating

level with mine as I woke to a distant sound
and wondered why its wings were not black.

*

My 20-year-old nephew yells at his mother
over the satellite phone.

They argue about his future when he returns,
but he doesn't want any advice.

Suddenly, he spits, "It is so bad here,
they are going to kill me any day!"

My mother recounts this when I ask her
how he is doing, insisting she told my sister

to ignore what he says under stress.
"It's his temper," my mother explains.

My nephew calls from Iraq every other day,
and everyone counts the months.

He is saving his soldier's pay
and sending it home.

At 18, he claimed he was serving his country
and used to say the Iraqis needed our help.

At 21, he says he doesn't know why he is there
and all his buddies want to come home.

                        *

The dragonfly of death hovers over water.
It is a perfect white in a blur of wings,

suspended over a huge, green leaf.
Why is it not black?

Distant voices send messages across the sea,
"I am okay," and I realize the dragonfly of death

is not an omen, but a seed lifted by wings
across dreams that try to understand why

the strange insect of another world, this world,
is the lone note left behind by the dead.

Yet, as I write this, I am wrong because I do
not know what the dragonfly means.

Soldier with a Book of Poems

The heartbeat in the stanzas keeps him alert.
The book smells new in the ruins and smoke.
When his earphones call, he puts the book in his pack.
When they hit the ground, the explosion sends him back.
Once, there was a book and a boy.
Twice, there was a rhyme about dogs and trees,
the way the river formed a place to rest.
If he could read the page, he would find
a dice cup held in the hands of his uncle,
who wanted to take a voyage, never return.
The poem reveals his uncle saving a company
of men by taking the enemy by surprise.
He flips through pages as the smoke clears,
finds the passage about errors of mercy, fruit
on dwarf trees, the way the poet imagined revenge
by hiding behind the shadows of a peasant girl.

The order is given and he runs, the book in his pack,
its pages crushed, an entry about one teardrop
blossoming into language anyone would fight over.
The engine in the stanzas keeps him against the wall
as he memorizes the last lines in one poem,
reciting without recognizing his buddy crouching
next to him—"Jose stepped into the light and
found the horse gasping for life, its glowing flanks
and shivering head pushing against the fence."
He stops saying the poem as things explode
around him, and it is written that the one who
carries a book of poems into battle follows
this moment, until the smoke clears
on the eyelids of his first lover, how he looked
down at her, long ago, without counting
the pages he had torn out of the book.

The Drowning

A man in an overcoat pointing
to thin ice on the lake.
A woman in red running across
a late-night movie screen.
The teenage couple lost in the forest,
a black house appearing through the trees.

The over-the-hill guitarist playing
his farewell tour as if he was still
a lifeguard doing air guitar in
the locker room of the local Y.
A bare arm rising out of the lake,
the legendary sword in its dripping hand.

Dead insects floating in the chlorine
of a backyard pool.
A glass pitcher of red Kool-Aid
falling off the kitchen table, shattering
into a thousand pieces as two boys
run out the door.

A car going over an icy bridge,
the lone driver surviving after
three weeks in the hospital.
A boy lying on a sandy beach, gasping
for air as the crowd spots the shark
fin circling beyond the waves.

A man in an overcoat following
car tracks until they vanish on thin ice.
The perfectly preserved warrior, dug up
in the tundra, containing an ancient
virus that slowly thaws on lab tables.

A cellar hiding a boy fascinated with
leaking pipes whose water freezes
into patterns near his feet.

The rescue of a four-legged animal
from a rushing river leading to a union
between its two rescuers, formerly strangers,
who meet in a stuffy motel two days
before the entire mountain town is
washed away in a historic flood.

Skyscraper Clothes

after John Ashbery

The rules of seeing can be learned by closing
the eyes and dividing the system into
loveable parts, regions of the world
where men have never been loved.

This angers the approach of the sparrows,
but the seeds have been waiting since
the last century, when music quit playing
and silence was involved in theories
about language, genuine voices,
and the investigation of the bare foot.

The crooked feet that survived were placed
in absentia by hands returning from the revolution.
This meant appearances were turned into
hours of thought where the groans
of many victims were recorded.

A party was held by closing the eyes
and multiplying desire against
the oldest relationships in memory.
Towels and white sheets were abandoned
in place of an obscure biography.

This may have overjoyed the ashen rain
that fell with ambition to tattoo smooth backs
and delivered a wet description of what happened—
a stranger, a harp player, and a public school
teacher erased a blackboard in time.

No one was loyal after the euphemism
and the criminal epidemic in the city.
No one sat down to create journeys in

notebooks, and no one wanted tea.
The rules never came into play after
words were forgotten, and beaten fires
in the alleys were put out by strange kisses.
No one has been able to figure out what
any of this means at this vertical point.

Comprehensible things going into the tall
buildings became collector's items in
the black hurricane of terror.
Crooked lines that survived the smoke
were placed in absentia by hands wanting
to sustain the urge to show mercy.

The end of this confusion was a constellation
that brought the tide without allowing
anyone to turn their backs on what happened
to those tall structures.
The party named in honor of the dead
never happened, and the walk home was
decorated with savage umbrellas
and the deepest well that ever disturbed
our clear and concise memories.
This results in the conclusion that mirrors
are subject to change, but no one stands
in front of one long enough to see that
the impossible is difficult to question,
though lines of doubt on our foreheads
continue to embrace fear.
Even the migration of the sparrows
between buildings chips at the stone
and brings the tools of disruption.

Hurl

We encountered the huge man
on our daily walk in the park.

He must have weighed 400 pounds,
lumbering out of his tiny car

to cross our path like he was
trying to get some exercise.

Suddenly, he leaned over a rusted
trash can and shivered, the awful

sound of his inner being thrashing
through his wide-open mouth,

the heaving roar scaring us,
making us quickly turn around in

the opposite direction, his vomiting
push one of the loudest sounds

from a human I have ever heard.
My wife walked faster as I looked

over my shoulder at the sick giant
twenty yards away, echoes of

his hurling wave amplified in
the drum of the trash can,

this enormous person appearing
out of nowhere to unravel before us,

reminding me I had the potential
to laugh or be frightened by his struggle,

the choking, dying instrument
that is fine-tuned at birth.

Fear of Dying

My student says the manuscript for her
first book is about the fear of dying.

She announces this as she reads poems
to a small audience that listens quietly.

I am startled because I have read the poems
without thinking they are about the fear of dying,

the window that strikes the light to become
something we encounter over and over.

I am surprised I overlooked it
and wonder if I missed it because

what I find in poems is what I have lived
in my lines about my grandmother

flying into my bedroom window on
the morning she passed away,

how I saw her for an instant, then
woke up knowing she was gone.

When a poet admits the fear of dying,
silence between words contains the river

she crossed, going there to find out
if what is being sought is the same

as what is written, wondering if
the lines that fill her pages are going

to stop the moment the window shuts
and the light stays in the room to change it.

On Many Readings

Wallace Stevens did everything to keep
from seeing how the dime glistened
in the air before landing in the grass.
When his wife appeared on the coin, it was
the image he chased for years, the lantern of
his mind caught on rice paper by Tu Fu
before his discovery of the path.

People are fleeing the rivers of birth.
When their children hold mapped globes
in their hands, curtains adorn the celebration
with something needing to be said—a distant
knocking converging in the head, an image
of the Himalayas not depth of field, but
the moment tracing syntax as a passage
read after the sound comes back.

Robert Lowell broke through the mist
and found the ocean, his white hair
spelling the way out of madness.
Each time he finished a line, the doves
on the sill outside his window paused
before rising into the air.
He noticed and scribbled shorter lines,
watched the birds through glass
and found a way to turn off the lamp.

Remastered

Bob Marley assigned three smoking gods
to his children, giving the spirits several years
to blanket the lights and weave a spell upon
his surviving band that played without him.
When Arthur Lee sang the entire *Forever Changes*
after 35 years, it was the first time the album was
completely performed on stage, its reincarnation
coming after years of drugs and breakdowns,
guns and the last dance with leukemia.
Robert Plant played at the benefit for Lee
four months before Love died, the gig
also marking the 30th anniversary of the death
of Plant's eleven-year-old son.
There are vaults of unreleased music Stevie
Ray Vaughn left after the helicopter went down,
Eric Clapton changing his mind about climbing
aboard at the last minute, the 25th anniversary
edition of *461 Ocean Boulevard* containing
a previously unreleased song about Clapton's
near-fatal overdose in a high-rise hotel
in London, a dark tower only seven blocks
from the apartment where Jimi Hendrix died.
Tim Buckley finally saw the dolphin he always
sang about when the needle melted his heart,
the white sea of destruction smacking his face
against the waves that also took his son Jeff
into the black fields under the river,
these drownings washing over the fact that
John Bonham and Keith Moon didn't waste
time when they beat their heavy drumsticks
against the doors of Heaven, only to find
the curtains of Hell in flames as their fans
illuminated the arena with thousands of cigarette
lighters held high in their bleeding hands.

Capricorn

after Max Ernst's sculpture Capricorn

The creature on his throne moves
his head of horns, his mouth frozen
in a perfect O because you stand in
front of a stone that has not fed on
anyone like you.
The huge, horned thing stares at you,
his tall staff waiting to pound you.
Perhaps, the museum guide is wrong
and the thing is peaceful and wants
to bless you so you can prosper.

The small thing in his arms
looks like a deformed baby cow,
its hanging tongue and round face
reminding you of a beached whale
that waits for you to make your move.
What are you afraid of?
Get closer, but watch for the trip
wires because electricity has taken
over and they love alarms.

There is something in the horned
mother's lap, perhaps the jar where
hospital staff threw your afterbirth
and told your mother to quit screaming.
The horns have moved a few times
since you have stood there.
You can't take the jar.
It could be a father.
Do fathers share their laps with sons?

To his left is the half woman–half beast,
horns, long neck, and two spread legs.
Why did Ernst sculpt this tower
of broken parts next to the grand
thing on the throne?
He lived for years in Arizona,
the birthplace of your mother.
Maybe he wanted to add to your
knowledge of stone and cliff,
sins with yellow dust hanging
all over your desert house.

Look at the two feet at the foot
of the twisted king,
the claws and the toes.
You must decide.
It can't be woman or man.
The feet are nearly hidden by
the cloak in the lap of the prince,
perhaps the thighs of a queen
holding her children for you
to dream about.
No wonder you were afraid
to leave your shoes at the door.

The Lives of Animals Are More than Multiplication

The lives of animals are more than multiplication.
This is true when the grasshopper enters your ear
or the bat lands in your hair and folds itself there,
thoughts of winged creatures so common these days,
the multiplication of flying shadows is a gift.
The lives of animals are beyond what we give
when a shark dives for a human leg
or the monkey comes back from the war
a decorated veteran that haunts the trees.

It can be part of the panda bear locked in the zoo,
the tiger that killed two young guys who taunted it,
its escape from the cage leading to its sacrifice
beyond the parrots up in the palms watching
the bloody scene go on, two or three parrots
at least seventy years old, the man who found
the first human victim wondering what it was
that left him last night when he awoke from
the dream of black snakes that climbed his legs
to warn him that there was one snake hiding in
his car tire and it was going to roll,

until the man arrived to release the bat from
his eyes and shoot the tiger.
This will be repeated because four poisonous
spiders dwell where the man can't see,
their time coming, their notion of what multiplies
so different from his thoughts, his face,
even his arm that hangs over the side of the bed
each time he closes his eyes and dreams that
more dinosaurs are becoming extinct.

—PART THREE—

Christmas Snow, Organ Mountains, New Mexico

Snow on the highest peaks that
cut through clouds like knives,
blades of rock colliding with white
shields above the desert.
Snow where there are roads,
white lanes on the mountain
where the climb is marked.

Inside one canyon, a white name for
elevation, the desert expanding as if
nothing like this has been seen before.
Tomorrow hidden in the mountain's
candle, embedded in the climber's torch,
the future ascending the canyon
as if ice can't keep up with
yesterday's light.

There is snow in the deepest arroyos,
waterfalls frozen in unkind shapes,
closed to this return,
hidden in clouds as if thinking
about loss is turning your back
on what is gained.

The Tarantulas

The tarantulas on the cliffs appear
out of the rocks each night,

their black dance moving down the walls in search
of a face that was carved from that stone.

The tarantulas on the cliffs appear as a nightly signal,
their swarm covering the earth like a man's beard,

the traces of tomorrow glistening on the rocks
the way the tarantulas spring at anything that moves,

at something that inhales
the desert air that has been breathed.

The tarantulas can feel a man's breath, even
sense where his body has slept, the cavern

at the bottom calling them to enter and
encircle him with one chance to look before

the air in his lungs becomes the thick hair
protecting his heart.

Ars Poetica

Even the sparrows don't know me.
I mistake my nightmares

for gifts from a god who is tired
of language, ideas, even resents

the image of a fat angel protecting
the world from its violent self.

When my nephew returned
from Iraq, he didn't sleep

for weeks, woke one night and
called his mother's name.

My sister did not answer because
she slept in the desert where

there are no names, dreaming
of the river we used to cross

as children, dreaming of a time
when all sons obeyed, though

many laid down to pretend
they were dead.

Even the snake grass is afraid of me.
I flatten it with my shoes and wish

I had grown up barefoot, though
I have not seen a rattler in decades

and wonder when a snake
last climbed up my bare arm

so I could study its rattles
and count the rings that

braced my heart with
the wisdom of sand.

Now, I see the reptilian
tattoos left behind by

young men who served.
Even my words are chosen

from a list hanging on the cottonwood
that used to guard the river.

When I yearn for the crossroads,
they never appear, and I ask the past

to bring scraps of bread to feed
mute sparrows that keep falling out

of my hair each turn I take
in answering my nightmares.

I Keep Listening

I keep listening to The Allman Brothers Band
and think back to the concert I saw in 1971,

two weeks before Duane Allman died.
I went to see them in Las Cruces, New Mexico,

with my best friend Bill, who disappeared from
the streets of our obsessions a few years later.

It was the last concert we saw together,
the last time we lit fires in the sweating crowd.

Now, I listen to "Whipping Post" and can't find him,
don't know where he lives or if he passes out drunk

as Duane and Dickey Betts light the stage
with two guitars—one scorching the endless road,

the other plugged into burning asphalt that marks
a highway exit toward the great comeback.

Relation

The seed grows into rare
desert skills where I follow
my deepest fears into the canyon
where no one emerges, the sacred
skirts of stone vanishing long ago.

Paradise is sand-blown, arriving
on the day I forgot how to
describe flowers, substituting
a fragment about astronomy
I chipped off the cliff house.

I come upon a dirt road
where an owl alights in
the middle of the desert night.
I stop before I can disturb it
and stare at the tiny, white
body that never moves.

River

If I gave away my country, there would be affection in the cities.
If I stumbled upon flags in the canyons, women in labor
would demand their sons return.
If I complied, you would lead me to the fountain
where Emiliano Zapata drank before his death.
If I wore the sombrero of stereotype, I would hide
inside the ovens where no one baked bread.
If I caught smoke from the mountain, animals
would become extinct and never find their way.
If I knew the difference between knowing and having,
I would take one word to find the wound of release,
my books dissolving to the touch.
If I convinced you that my habits were things to come,
you would reward me with guitars on street corners
where intensive care is spray-painted on the bricks.

If I gave away my country, there would be flesh in the cities.
If I released my rivals to consume the playgrounds,
they would pockmark the chairs of their fathers with
sweat poured from things they could never say.
If I waited to say them myself, my dogs would seize
their prey and never obey me again.
If I cut open a head of lettuce to find the worm,
the fields would no longer let me stand.
If I came home to rearrange my hair, I would be
the first bald son to make it back.
If I stopped to acknowledge the impaled
snake on the fence, no one would believe me,
only say, "Enough is enough," and lead me
to a waiting truck full of desperate men.

After Touching the Forehead

This light tracing the chair came
from the other side of sleep where

the prowler visited with a cold knife
and his sister hugged a man she didn't love.

This warmth on my fingers
is a way of being chosen.

It leads my hand to a bruise on my hip
I didn't notice before.

It makes the caraganda
in the garden stand up.

This perfect sleep is a lie,
a story between learning and dreaming

of the wild rabbit in the yard chewing
the leaves before leaping away.

These mutterings are simple in their silence,
the way the Navajo blanket deceives the body.

Not out of dream, but love.
Not out of love's curve, but the cost
of uncovering it in the morning.

One in Three

One in three flasks as if the rain
is falling before the cave.

One in three a scene that doesn't
recall it is there—how you have hidden

the bell in outstretched hands that
mistook trees for people.

Blue stars never seen, the empty
flower smoothing the moment

of descent, thumb staying
ahead of the reptilian glare.

When it flies home,
the crow is a saint.

When it lands to disappear, one in
three flasks contains the leaf.

Last Night

Last night I thought the Martians came.
Don't laugh.

It was only me, waking from a dream
where my father was dying,

spinning out of the heavens to ask forgiveness
for staying up there too long.

Last night, I was his son, and he lifted me
in his arms before he hit the earth.

The explosion was amazing, and I woke up
with a beard on my face.

Last night, I slept as if I were
the last man in the family,

an old, confused stranger trying
every locked door, unable to get in.

I kept sleeping when the man finally
entered through the broken window,

shards of glass in his hair
as blinding as the stars.

If by Chance, the Child Prodigy

The northern stars demand that
the southern stars go home.
Instructions say the planets
should not be written about
unless the child prodigy is there,
resurrected as a thought in
a handwritten note dropped
on a school playground.
The telegram floats like a guide
to the burial sites and the color of
the eyes that sit in their skulls.
The northern stars draw closer,
and the galaxy changes into
a pie plate used by a pioneer
woman in a rotting cabin on
the plains of Nebraska in 1882.

It was a voyage intended for love,
but clouds over the territories
prevented such a thing.
The southern stars realign
the black hole as the universe
intended—no dark star in
the root of all things.
Pursued with Venus and Pluto,
the buffalo herd makes it
across the continent.
If by chance the child prodigy
slices a meteor with her mind,
this will not take place.
Men will climb down
stone steps to have a look.
Star charts will be abolished,
and contaminated gardens
will take their place.

The northern hand grasps
the southern hand, and the smell
between them floats eastward.
The western reaches do not
shake hands with approaching
civilizations, canyons,
unused wooden weapons,
or worn sandals,
even the empire at rest.
Women run up the stone
steps because they have
no reason to look.
If by chance the child prodigy
traces a blood canal in her
spinal cord, the tribe
will be changed.
Devastations will thrive
in perfect silence.
Linear ideas and lessons
will be perceived.
The fury created by such
a philosophy will raise
casualties, and the nation
will pull out of the country
where the coffins thrive.
Eastern constellations shall
outnumber western nebulas,
though the path of the starship
was plotted in the books
eight thousand years ago.

Children in dusty schoolrooms,
textbooks turning yellow
on shelves against back walls,
cults and believers presenting
Web sites for tracking the northern

and southern stars.
If by chance the child prodigy
survives the cluster bomb,
let her walk again, because
her bloody feet can still
move across the ground
without renaming the earth.

Enduring Imagination

No one can be accused of framing me on their wall.
This means the stain in the heart took place on
one afternoon of rain and disemboweled butterflies,
ideas structured around a system designed to fool
friends and increase the number of my enemies.
When Federico García Lorca woke in a bed of leaves,
it was the wrong world and he would not write about it.
Instead, he sang a song for the morning they came for him,
the lyrics hidden in a glass of wine on the windowsill.

No one can identify the path to the waterfall
because streams of thought have disappeared.
No one can say I was at fault because I was whispering
to someone about a teacher I once had, how he lined up
empty bottles of Coke to keep from drinking fire again,
his poems bristling with a redemption song, a quick
turn away from the darkness dripping in the mist.
When WC Williams brought another child into the world,
he washed his hands in a tiny sink, the first cries of
tomorrow giving him lines for a poem he would never write.
Instead, a woman he fell in love with walked in the door
and told him to place his hands on her breasts.

The Gift

for Ida

He brought her a gift that
was never meant to be opened.
It would be seen as the swan
slanting its bill.
He brought her a box that
circled the stairs, then floated
above her outstretched arms.
It would be noted that it was preserved
in glass, and the boys were
shirtless when they found
the box on the bed.
He brought her to a door
ignored during the lunar eclipse,
but she had been there before,
her visit so generous, his life's
wages were lost before the war.
He brought her a word that
sounded like the wind in the trees,
the rustling of doubt that gave them
a moment to look at the stones
aligned by someone who wanted
to make sure their path led
away from the tree.
He brought her back from
the splendors of nature,
didn't know what to do about
her wishes, how they translated
heaven into a ceremony for
old lovers who knew how to get
out of the world by staying

where they were.
They brought each other
the passion of the double hearts,
desire bristling among familiar
footsteps on the night when they
gave away what they wanted before
morning caught them perfectly still.

The Fold

You have not made origami,
but a simple fold, the paper
crackling into hidden corners
that equal a pattern
you have loved since
you were a child—
a familiar geometry
as insulated as the way
you tuck your feet under
the blanket and go to sleep.

You have bent dimensions
into unsolved parallels,
the music as transparent
as a vast current that holds
the crease of your feelings
against a brilliant portrait
where people emerge as
flat wheels that fold into
time hung on the walls.

You have not folded them yet,
but they are there—the line
you must crease bending
inside itself to fold into
a secret you can't reveal
until the earth becomes as
flat as a dead man lying in
the parlor, his family grieving
because the stiff body refused
to fold its hands together.

Fathers and Sons

He said, "My father
is a frog."

I said, "The enemy is
the cool butterfly."

He wondered, "Has my father
jumped too far?"

I answered, "Your friend is
the caterpillar before wings."

What Do You See?

"What do you see?" he asked
himself and stared through
the grove of cottonwoods
until something settled behind
the huge leaves.
When he looked again, he was
someone he hadn't been in years.
He dug in the mud until
his shoes were covered,
then gripped the fossil
in his hands.

"What do you think is there?"
he asked in the voice
of an old friend.
He rubbed dirt off the shell
and stared at the tiny ribs.
When something moved again
in the trees, he saw what it was.
He stepped forward and took
it and never spoke in
the voice of another.

"What do you see?" his son
once asked him as the boy
ran across the playground
to be pushed by other boys.
He watched them become
men by staying away late
and never telling what they did.
When the cottonwoods
moved in the wind, he gazed

into the setting sun that
made him squint, tears
of light running down his
cheeks, because it was never
too late for a blind man
to finally see.

The Word

Now the word is done
and the ground searches for shoes.
Over four thousand dead are no match
for a nightmare in a desert farther
than the nearest chair.

The word is an anvil pounded
through the clouds, hoping to
absorb the rain that holds back
the rumor of peace implanted
in the back of the neck.

Now the word is done
and shadows are loved during
the morning of prayer mistaken
for a poem angry at a world that
brings flowers and birds.

The word is gray with
goodness and transforms
smoke into a painting
absent of the human soul.

Now the word is silent
and the table searches for milk,
follows the lines until
speech is given to the first hand
that dots a small "i."

The word is done as the ground
searches for white space
no one writes on because
thousands of pages resist the hand.

Fragment

Listen.
The guitar has stopped.

You are safe.
The white beard is gone.

There is a window full of
birds and a glass of water.

Please listen.
The guitar has fallen.

The hard floor makes
the strings vibrate.

You are singing and
the white figure is gone.

There is a song
you used to know,

but the homebound train
took it decades ago.

Listen.
The instrument you have been

making lies on your table.
You must touch it again

before its intricate shape
disappears.

The Stone Ring, Las Truchas, New Mexico

I saw it on the cliff above me
the last time I climbed.

The stone ring was a circle whose
red shape was cracked and worn,

tree limbs growing through it, circular
erosion sending me higher with

the fear of falling, not able to put
one arm through the hole and

convince myself it was a natural shape,
not something carved by a lone man

who looked down when the sun set,
raised his head each morning when

light formed its red cycle that
gave him time to be here.

I hung onto the cliff edge, felt the pull at
my legs and closed my eyes as I touched

the roundness of it, moved pebbles aside
to try and read fading lines the man left,

his symbols a message that marked altitudes
I should not have reached, the point

where he went too far, my trembling
fingers tracing a reply I had not

spelled since I was a boy.
The words were eroded into a ring

that fit what I wanted to believe,
things I had not shared with anyone,

a circular motion that held me up there
as if I deserved it, my fingers stained in red

from rubbing on the circle as I crushed
a few inches of it in my hands.

I descended guilty with clouds, rich with dirt
that did not belong to me, yet tasted like

the earth when I cleaned my fingertips by
licking them with my tongue.

And by the Eagles that Peck at Me

And by the eagles that peck at me,
I wake, bend to the river and drink.
I grow old and see the mountain for what it is.

I escape barefoot, reach the sea and bow to pray,
find my limping father coming toward me,
wrinkled and full of regret.

And by those eagles, the rattlesnake crawls,
wishing it could reach me and strike my heart as
illegal men cross to this side to share pieces of meat.

I eat grains of dirt instead, the crunching sound
of my new tongue burning in the sun
for not being taught the word for *house*.

And by those eagles, I am given a rattle,
a book that won't open until I write it,
my ancestors rising to act out what I have written.

And by those feathers, my mother gives birth
to a brother I never knew, then buries something
in the sand without looking at me.

Years later, I dig it up, surprised the secret is still there
so I can turn on my captors and feed on them.
And by the eagles that peck at me in return, I am freed.

Acknowledgments

The author would like to thank the following publications, where some of these poems first appeared:

Acentos Review: "And by the Eagles that Peck at Me" and "My City Is Full of Insects"

Aspects of Robinson: Homage to Weldon Kees (University of Nebraska Press, 2009): "Not Today"

Bad Mother Chronicles: "Allen Ginsberg's Mother"

Barrow Street: "Skyscraper Clothes"

Bitter Oleander: "The Fold," "The Lives of Animals Are More than Multiplication," and "The Poem of One Hundred Tongues"

Bombay Gin: "Faith Run"

Burnside Review: "Chosen"

Elixir: "One in Three"

Fine Unraveling: "Awake"

Hayden's Ferry Review: "The Shortest Poem"

Indiana Review: "After Touching the Forehead," "Capricorn," and "Juárez Bees"

Konundrum: "Ears Full of Thorns"

Lake Effect: "Honking at the Cemetery"

Literary El Paso (TCU Press, 2009): "Somewhere Outside El Paso" and "The Rio Grande Near Flood Stage, Summer 2006"

Prairie Schooner: "Chosen" and "Finished House"

Refined Savage Poetry Review: "Enduring Imagination" and "The Word"

Solo Cafe: "Fear of Dying" and "The Long Library"

Superstition Review: "If by Chance, the Child Prodigy"

Two Review: "The Stone Ring, Las Truchas, New Mexico," "Photo of Pablo Picasso with His Shirt Off," "Bob Dylan in El Paso, 1963," and "Reading: Late Summer"

2008 Poetry Calendar (Alhambra Publishing): "Chimayo, New Mexico"

2009 Poetry Calendar (Alhambra Publishing): "On Many Readings"

About the Author

Ray Gonzalez is the author of ten books of poetry, including five from BOA Editions—*The Heat of Arrivals* (winner of a 1997 PEN/Oakland Josephine Miles Book Award), *Cabato Sentora* (finalist for the 2000 Minnesota Book Award), *The Hawk Temple at Tierra Grande* (winner of a 2003 Minnesota Book Award for Poetry), *Consideration of the Guitar: New and Selected Poems* (2005), and the forthcoming *Cool Auditor* (2009). *Turtle Pictures* (University of Arizona Press, 2000), a mixed-genre text, received the 2001 Minnesota Book Award for Poetry. His poetry has appeared in the 1999, 2000, and 2003 editions of *The Best American Poetry* (Scribners) and in *The Pushcart Prize: Best of the Small Presses 2000* (Pushcart Press). He is also the author of three collections of essays: *Memory Fever* (University of Arizona Press, 1999), a memoir about growing up in the Southwest; *Renaming the Earth: Personal Essays* (University of Arizona Press, 2008); and *The Underground Heart: A Return to a Hidden Landscape* (University of Arizona Press, 2002), which received the 2003 Carr P. Collins/Texas Institute of Letters Award for Best Book of Nonfiction, was named one of ten Best Southwest Books of the Year by the Arizona Humanities Commission, was named one of the Best Nonfiction Books of the Year by the *Rocky Mountain News*, was named a Minnesota Book Award Finalist in Memoir, and was selected as a Book of the Month by the El Paso Public Library. He has written two collections of short stories: *The Ghost of John Wayne* (University of Arizona Press, 2001), winner of a 2002 Western Heritage Award for Best Short Story and a 2002 Latino Heritage Award in Literature, and *Circling the Tortilla Dragon* (Creative Arts, 2002). His second mixed-genre text, *The Religion of Hands* (volume two of the *Turtle Pictures* trilogy) was published by the University of Arizona Press in 2005. He is the editor of twelve anthologies, most recently *No Boundaries: Prose Poems by 24 American Poets* (Tupelo Press, 2002). He has served as poetry editor of *The Bloomsbury Review* for twenty-two years and founded *LUNA*, a poetry journal, in 1998. He is a professor in the MFA Creative Writing Program at the University of Minnesota in Minneapolis and also teaches in the Solstice Low-Residency MFA Program at Pine Manor College in Boston.

Library of Congress Cataloging-in-Publication Data

González, Ray.
  Faith run : poems / by Ray González.
    p. cm.—(Camino del sol: a Latina and Latino
literary series)
  ISBN 978-0-8165-2769-4 (pbk. : alk. paper)
  1. Landscape—Southwest, New—Poetry. 2. Southwest,
New—Poetry. 3. Mexican-American Border Region—Poetry.
I. Title.
  PS3557.O476F34 2009
  811'.54—dc22   2009007237